For George
a new
with best wishes
Ellen Hudson

A Tennessee Tale as told by ...

Felix

Ellen W. Hudson

This is the place for me to state that the names and characters used in this narrative are purely fictitious and any resemblance to persons living or dead is purely coincidental. However, this is not the case. A great many of the names do refer to actual persons ... it is only the ones which might possibly offend in some way that are fictitious!

E. W. H.

ISBN 0-9642859-0-8

© Copyright 1994. Full Circle Publishing Company.
All rights reserved.

I wish to dedicate this book to my cousin, Ann, who helped me "remember," to those in the Monday Writers group who gave me encouragement, and, of course, to Tom who makes everything I do possible.

Felix Harrison Badger
1869 - 1964

Come in here, young fellow. I'm always glad to meet a new neighbor. What'd you say your name was? Well, Jacob, my name's Felix and I can remember when I was a lad about your age. Things were sure different, though, when I was coming along. How come? Well, ...

One

    I never could understand how Ma could stomach having Rip around after he killed my Pa. I couldn't get along with him no matter how I tried. He was lazy, mean, and cantankerous but I reckon Ma figured she had to put up with him or else give up the farm and live on the kindness of neighbors. I know now that without that old mule the two of us could never have put in the garden that fed us or tend the corn we sold to old Sam Crenshaw, the miller. But the day Rip kicked Pa in the head while he was bending over to pick up his hat the wind had blowed off I wanted to get down the gun and shoot that danged animal. Ma and me brought Pa in and laid him out on the cherry bed I still sleep on, but he was already dead. Ma never shed a tear...just straightened her back and set her mouth in that thin line that showed me she was working to overcome something in her that she didn't want to come out. Then she started in to talking in that same tone of voice she used when she was fixing Pa's breakfast and naming off the chores that had to be done before sundown...but she wasn't talking to me...just sorta tossing words out into thin air. That was when I got that sour, coppery taste in my mouth and drug the split-bottom chair over to the hearth to get down Pa's gun.

"No, Felix," was all she said, and I got right down off the chair. It never dawned on me to ask "why", much less go against her. You just didn't talk back to Ma. Even Pa never questioned her and I don't recall anyone ever doing anything anyway but the way she wanted it done. It wasn't that she was bossy. She just had a way about her that made you think she knew exactly what she was about.

Now Pa, he had a looseness about him. I can still bring up pictures in my mind of him, leaning on the hoe, laughing at the the puppy chasing its tail. When Pa laughed you couldn't hear him...just see his shoulders shaking and wait for him to get out his bandana to wipe the tears away. He used to cry over pretty things, too...like the time when we was hunting and came up on that young doe, tripping along like a fine lady, coming out of the mist that was rising along the edge of the woods. But don't get the idea he was a weak man. Anything but. No one could work a forty-seven acre farm with no help but a skinny boy and a mule and be called "weak". It was just that he seemed to see into things that other folks only looked at. Maybe since I worked alongside him till I was twelve, some of his ways rubbed off on me. I don't know. But yesterday, right after the sun went down behind the sycamore grove and the whole sky turned that rosy pink like it does sometimes in the early winter, I caught myself reaching for my handkerchief ....

Two

    Belle was born when I was six. Ma had a couple of stillborns between us so when Mrs.Lewis,the midwife from over near Mountain Creek, told us that this one was a strong and lusty girl we had a celebration! Pa unhitched Rip and shoo-ed him out to the pasture and got down the cider jugs ... one he used to fill his and Mrs. Lewis' cups and one he used for mine. Even Ma got to chuckling over Pa's tales of what Belle would grow up to be like and how he'd teach her to ride a horse (he didn't say where that horse would come from) and how Ma would teach her to make brown betty. Long after Mrs. Lewis left, we were still sitting there all together, watching Ma nurse the baby, and listening to Pa tell stories that got harder and harder to believe with each fresh cup of cider ... it was a happy time.

    But Belle didn't live long enough to do all those things Pa had talked and dreamed about. One day, when she was about nine months old,she was playing on the floor while Ma patched my good shirt, and she swallowed a button that had fallen out of Ma's mending basket. We figure that's what musta happened cause later we counted the buttons Ma had just bought to go on the new dress she was making to wear to church on Easter, and one was missing. You know, Ma says Belle didn't make any noises 'cept what was natural for a happy baby ... says she just looked over and there she was, turning blue, and by then turning her upside down didn't do any good ... she was dead by the time Ma's hollering brought Pa in from the corn rows.

Ma didn't cry. But I watched her droop like the spring beauties do when a late frost catches them out in the open, and I know this sounds sorta strange, but she got to be an old lady overnight. Oh, I don't mean her hair turned snow white or anything, but she never again walked straight up and proud like she once did. Now Pa, HE cried. He wouldn't (or couldn't) help Ma and me dig the grave or hammer together the little coffin, and the next day when we buried Belle, Ma had to say the twenty-third psalm even though Pa was always the one who insisted on reading from the Good Book every night and who made me say three new Bible verses every Sunday. Ma and me found a rock in the woods that was sorta shaped like a cross and scratched her name on it, but Pa was the one who found the prettiest flowers to put on her grave every Saturday night after quitting time. Now don't worry. Belle's grave's not still there at the edge of the woods where you can see the pigs rootin'. We moved her five years later when the church at Mt. Pisgah was built and we fenced in the graveyard there. You've seen that graveyard, haven't you? Folks from away from here who see it for the first time seem to think it's sorta unusual, so I guess if you have seen it you remember that the graves are covered with two slabs of stone, sitting up like a tent, with little cedar trees planted at each end. Well, the one you see in our row that's only about two feet long ... that's Belle.

By the way ... I still have that little cross-shaped rock. I use it to keep the wind from banging the door back and forth, and Ma's mending basket still sits on the sugar chest in the hall. We weren't brought up to throw away useful things ... besides, painful memories sometime keep us from taking the happy times for granted.

Three

After we lost Belle things went along about the same on the farm. I guess I carried a right smart load for a little fella even before Pa died. He was away from home a lot cause he was the only tooth doctor in the county. Oh, he didn't go off to school to learn to be a doctor ... he just followed Dr. Smallman around a lot, and when Dr.Smallman died he left Pa his pliars and things, so folks started calling Pa when they had a tooth go rotten or something. They would give him money when he pulled their teeth or eased a toothache with a poultice of yarrow leaves, and this helped out considerably, specially in the years when we had a poor crop year. It sure made me proud when we'd walk in church and I'd hear someone call out, "Hi,Doc." Now the only REAL doctor in our neck-of-the-woods was Dr.Hudson and he would occasionally call Pa in to help him cause he knew Pa was used to the sight of blood and wouldn't go water-kneed on him.

But, listen to me! Seems like ever time I go to tell you something I start rambling on about Pa. Guess he musta put his mark on me pretty deep in those twelve years we were around together. I had started out to tell you about how I met Ellen. Once I was big enough to take on a few chores, Ma told me it was my job to see that the fire in the kitchen range never went out. I suppose people in town had sulfa matches in those days but we didn't, and if the fire went out I had to walk about a mile over to the Cantrells and bring a live coal home in a bucket. I wasn't lazy, but I didn't always keep my mind on my business ... even then! ... and many's the time I made that trek across to the neighbor's. You'd think I'd have learned after a time or two, but maybe deep down I liked that walk across the fields and through the woods, jumping gullies and calling up Bob-whites, stopping to cut a pea shooter in the cane brake, or catching a little garter snake to scare the Cantrell girls with. Anyway, one early April morning Ma called up to tell me I'd done it again ... so I muttered something under my breath that she would have snatched me bald for saying if she'd heard me, pulled on my britches and heavy shirt (we were having one of those cool snaps that keep breaking in on spring, either "dogwood winter" or "locust winter" ... can't remember which), got my bucket and started out. As I walked along the creek bank I noticed the dog-toothed violets were in bloom, so I picked some for Mrs. Cantrell. That woman craved pretty things and I was hoping she'd be pleased enough to fix me some breakfast as Ma hadn't exactly been in a frame of mind to cater to me that morning, especially since she had no stove to cook on!

When I walked in their cabin, carrying the bunch of little yellow flowers, I saw another gal sitting at the table with Amy and Lucy Cantrell. She couldn't have been more than six years old, but as she sat there in that room full of people I couldn't see any one but her. The early morning slanted sun came in the door with me and lit on the brightest head of long red curls I ever saw, and her big brown eyes looked at me for only a flicker before they dropped to the posies I carried. "What pretty trout lilies", she said and I would have no more have corrected her than I would have corrected Ma. I'm glad I didn't, 'cause even then he knew more about growing things than most anyone else around our way. Turns out her family lived next to the Boyds, and old Mr. Boyd took a shine to that little girl with so many questions about the plants he was growing to sell to people, and he got a kick out of teaching her all about trees and flowers and bushes and even their Latin names.

Anyway, it seems she had come over to the Cantrell's with her Pa who had come to trade mules with Ben ... that's what Mr. Wilson did for a living, trade horses and mules ... and he and Ellen had spent the night, it being too late to start home after the men finished their haggling. Now it would be nice to say I hung around a while to enjoy Ellen's company but I must own up to the fact that she sorta rubbed me the wrong way that morning, being so know-it-all about the flowers, so as soon as I'd had my hot buttered grits and biscuits (Mrs. C. did appreciate the bouquet) I headed on home with the red hot coal. Ten more years had gone round the bend before I saw her again, but now I look back on it, I never called trout lilies "dog toothed violets" again!

Four

The next few years after Pa died will not go down in my book as "happy times." Ma and me worked like six people, trying to keep the farm going and all the time Ma getting crankier and tighter lipped. About this time I started shooting up, tall as a lombardy and, with precious little meat to stretch over the bones, I ended up being right skinny. There wasn't much empty time to be found in those days but it seemed like I had to get off by myself ever now and then and do a little thinking (or day dreaming or whatever you want to call it). When Ma would fall asleep over her mending after supper, I'd slip out and head for the woods or follow the creek down to where the wood ducks nested. Sometimes I got to go with a clear conscience like when Ma sent me looking for tansy for her rheumatism tea or red clover for feet-itch poultices.

I don't know where in tarnation Ma learned all she knew about cures and potions but, living in the country like we did, her know-how came in mighty handy. Like the time I fell out of the tree I had climbed to rob the bees' honey hole and broke my leg right above the ankle. I actually heard it crack and I musta screamed something awful cause Ma came running hell-for-Sunday and me over half a mile from home! Anyway, she got Rip and somehow got me up on him and home, and after she gave me a piece of leather harness to bite on, she jerked my leg till it popped back like it was supposed to lay. I guess I passed out cause the next I knowed I was in bed and Ma had wet burdock leaves packed around my leg to keep the swelling down and was covering that with damp red clay. Then she wrapped it with brown paper and told me if I dared to move before it all dried, my leg would heal crooked. You can bet your bottom dollar I never twitched so much as a muscle for most of that day, and I want you to know that several months later, when Ma took the hammer and chipped off the clay, my broken leg was ever bit as straight as my good one! course it was a little bit skinnier, but after I had worked in the fields for a few weeks, you couldn't tell which one I had broke.

As I know now, her healings and treatings were about half superstition. Like the time one of the Cantrell girls was bit by a wild dog while she was walking home from school and Mrs. Cantrell got in a tissie 'cause she just knew the dog had to be "mad." She came to Ma looking for a "mad stone" 'cause Ma's success with cures had made a name for her around the countryside. Well, Ma didn't have one but she knew an old woman over near Woodbury that did, so she, Mrs. Cantrell and little Amy got in the wagon and took off.

When they got back late that night and dropped Ma off at our house, I asked Ma what in tarnation was a "mad stone". She told me that there was this certain rock, actually a bloodstone, that was shaped like a dog's ear, and you were supposed to tie it on the bite with a length of plaited corn silk. Once it fell off, you put it in a bowl of sweet milk and if the milk turned sour it meant the stone had drawed off the poison.

I asked her what if the milk stayed sweet and she just smiled and said, "no one's ever found out!"

Hello, there, Jacob. What you selling? Sure, I'll take one. Always was one to encourage free enterprise. Must say, though, things come a lot easier to your generation than they did to mine.

Five

I guess I thought Ma and Me would go on forever, with us sharing the chores and me going to school whenever I could take the time away from the farming, but I was living in dream world. I didn't think a lot about it when Dr.Cope started coming home with us after church to eat dinner ... just assumed he was tired of eating his own cooking since his wife had died of consumption and everybody knew Ma made the best chicken and dumplings in the whole county. So when Ma came and sat on the side of my bed in the loft one night and told me she was going to marry that man, you could have knocked me over with a feather. To this very day I can call up that picture in my mind ... me, lying there in my nightshirt with my long skinny legs and knobby knees hanging out, and Ma patting my arm to try and soften what she musta known would be a real blow to me. It was summer ... probably July, cause I remember looking out the window to hide my wet eyes and seeing lightning bugs and I remember hearing a whipoorwill somewhere off in the distance, and for a long time neither of us said a word. Then Ma set in to talking and saying things like, "I just know you'll learn to like your new Pa" and "Things will go on just the same as they always have." I didn't say anything, partly because of the lump in my throat and partly because I was busy planning how I would make out on my own, cause I knew I could never live in the same house with that man or watch Ma cook and clean for him and share her bed with him.

I suppose I never gave a thought to how it would hurt Ma (young folks are so self-centered and I was sure no different from the most), but early next morning, long before daylight had outlined the cottonwood trees that grew along the east side of the pasture, I tied a few clothes up in a gunnysack, grabbed some cornbread and an apple or two from the kitchen and walked away from the only home I'd ever known.

I often wonder what it would've been like had I stayed on, but I really don't know of too many things about my life I would have changed if given the chance. I do know that those first fifteen years, living and working on the farm with Pa and Ma, molded me in ways I no more could've changed than I could have made the creek run up our hill instead of down.

As things worked out I ended up working for Mr. Gribble in his store over in Dibrell and living in a room he built on off to one side. Mr. Gribble had a place in the back of the store where he sold "drugs" (as they had started calling the cures and potions made up to help those who were feeling poorly) and when he found out how much I had picked up by going with Pa when he rode out to tend someone with a toothache and from helping Ma gather roots and plants for her teas and poultices, he put me to work in that section and pretty soon those who came in got to asking my advice about what would help them feel better and 'fore long I was rolling pills and crushing powders and had taken over that part of the business. Somewhere I still have a fancy looking certificate they gave me, calling me a "pharmacist" and making it legal to do what I'd been doing for about five years!

From time to time Mr. Wilson came by the store to pick up supplies. Sometimes he'd have a few of his children with him and occasionally just Ellen would come in with her little brothers and sisters ... seemed like it took them an hour just to choose which piece of penny candy each one wanted ... so I got to know the family pretty well. One day, after a right smart spell had gone by without them coming in, the screen door slammed and when I looked up to see who it was, the late afternoon sun lit on those red curls and my stomach felt like it did the time my friend, Bill Mooneyhan, hit me there when we were fooling around and feeling our oats. I later found out she had been going to the Female Academy over in McMinnville for a couple of years and it seemed she had grown into a young lady overnight. When she smiled and said, "Afternoon, Felix" my mouth got so dry I couldn't do a thing but grin and simper like somebody without good sense. She was the prettiest thing I ever laid eyes on and I felt like I wanted to "eat her up" ... and as some of you have heard me say, "many's the time I wished I had"!

Thinking I was only bashful, she then took over the better part of the conversation (nothing about that changed much over the years!) and after she left I was walking around without my feet touching the ground and Mr. Gribble had to tell me three times it was time to close up before I realized he was talking to me. As they say nowadays, I had fallen like a "ton of bricks" and after that I spent more time than was seemly wondering when I'd see those big brown eyes again.

I started calling on Ellen and the Wilsons seemed to tolerate my hanging around pretty well, so I naturally commenced to thinking about asking her to marry me. The idea of having a family of my own was especially appealing to me as I had been denied that pleasurable state for a long time. Oh, I'd go by and see Ma ever once in a while but with her new crop of children and Dr. Cope always around, I never felt quite like I belonged. Being on my own for so long had made me grow up in a hurry so the only concern I had about getting tied up with a family was money. I knew I'd have to find us a house to live in before I went to see Mr. Wilson, as that room off Mr. Gribble's store just wouldn't "cut the mustard". Well, pretty soon I found the very place I was looking for. It had only one drawback ... it was about seven miles down the road towards Sparta and we'd have to have the means to get back and forth to town. As my needs and wants had been very meager these past few years I had saved up enough to pay for the house so I went ahead and popped the question, feeling that the Lord would provide the answer to my problem if He thought I was deserving of having Ellen become my bride.

It'll come as no surprise to you that she agreed to be Mrs. Badger but what might surprise you is how the Lord responded. One day, only two weeks later, Mr. Smartt, who somehow seemed to know everything that was going on in the county, came in the store saying that Miss Mattie Bell, the school teacher, had to go up north to New York State to nurse her sister who had had an accident, and they needed someone to take charge of the schoolhouse for the summer and to be sure the children didn't get too far behind in their lessons. Mr. Smartt had all of us dying laughing while he told about Miss Mattie's sister, who weighed over two hundred pounds, falling upside down in their new rain barrel and having to call in three strange men off the street to help pull her out, and all the while the sister was yelling bloody murder about not wanting strangers to see her everyday drawers that had a split in the seam! He declared it must have been all the screaming and squirming that caused her to wrench her back so bad she had to be put to bed. With that everyone in the store started making shady remarks about the poor lady's upside down condition and wondering how Miss Mattie, who weighed ninety-eight pounds wringing wet would be able to do anything for her bedridden patient but wait on her and listen to her whine.

Well, I didn't waste much time worrying about Miss Mattie or her sister and as soon as I could break in without seeming rude, I asked how much the job would pay, and when Mr.Smartt said twenty-five dollars for two months I asked Mr.Gribble if I could take time off in the mornings to teach so long as I tended the store in the afternoons and did the pill rolling, as well as the cleaning up, after closing time. Now, Mr.Gribble kinda looked on me as a son and he had a soft spot for Ellen, too, so he was nice enough to say "yes." He was also nice enough not to ask how in tarnation I thought I could teach others what I might not have been taught myself. But I had always carried the notion that I could do most anything I set my mind to ... Pa had taught me that and Ma had given me plenty of opportunities to test it! ... so I spent that summer going over multiplication tables as I mopped floors and boning up on history dates as I pulverized powders. Reading came easy to me, as did memory work, as a result of all that Bible study Ma and I got into after supper at night, and clerking in the store made mathematics seem second nature to me. As for all the rest, I learned from books at night what I taught the children the next day. I had to pretend to know it all, even if I didn't, cause some of those students were almost as old as I was and many of the boys outweighed me ... though none looked down on me! That was a wonderous two months. Never again would I take lightly just what an education can mean to a man, or for that matter, to the children he brings into the world. Throughout my life I've held the conviction that a body can never know all there is to know but he can add daily to his store of knowledge by listening and looking in the most unlikely places. I'll tell you for a fact that that summer those kids taught me a lot more than I taught them.

Six

When That summer was over and they paid me the twenty-five dollars I felt as rich as any man ever felt and I wasted no time in hopping over to Mr.Lively's livery stable to see about buying a horse.As I walked in I bumped square into Mr.Wilson who had come by to take orders and trade talk with the older men who always sat around in back playing checkers.When I explained my mission he told me he had his eye on a little filly over in West Tennessee that he planned on buying and giving to us as a wedding gift, but that I might like to take a look at the new buggy Mr.Lively had just gotten in. Well, I fell in love on the spot! That was the prettiest, sportiest little shiny black carriage you would ever hope to see. It even had its spokes painted with red stripes! It didn't take much imagination to picture Ellen all dressed up and sitting there beside me, driving to Sunday services, and our being the envy of all the neighbors. Now, I was no innocent when it came to the Biblical warnings about pride and covetousness, but I let my heart take over from my head and I handed over my earnings and promised a few more paychecks and right then and there became the proud owner of a new buggy.

By this time I had moved into the house on the Sparta road and was trying to spruce it up a bit before our wedding in December ... (Mrs.Wilson had said she couldn't possibly get Ellen's trousseau together before then, but why she thought Ellen would need a lot of fancy clothes just to live out in the country with a poor young fella like me, I couldn't figure. Maybe she could see down the road aways to where we would sit a little higher on the community ladder.) One of the first things I did after Mr.Lively had my new purchase towed out to the house was to build on a lean-to shed to protect it from the weather. I was sure proud of that buggy and went out every morning before going in to work to polish the shiny finish and to be sure the swallows hadn't roosted above it overnight.

My "come-uppance" was not long in coming up. I was sound asleep one night in mid-October when I suddenly became aware of that soft, eerie silence you "hear" when the whole world around you is blanketed with a new snowfall. I looked out, and in the light of a three-quarter moon, I could see the big maple tree beside my window, leaves still clinging to its limbs, bending almost double with their heavy burden.In that light it seemed to my eyes that the leaves underneath the snow were tinting the whole tree with a rosy, other-worldly glow so that it looked like a giant head of Joe-Pye-Weed, and I was still standing there, marveling at God's handiwork, when I heard a terrible crash and then and there witnessed His awesome power. The sheer weight of the snow piled on the leaf-laden branches had split the huge tree from tip to toe and one of the largest limbs landed smack dab on top of the new shed. When I ran outside I saw in a minute that my "pride" had surely "gone before destruction" and my "haughty spirit" before a "fall!" The lean-to was a shambles and the beautiful little buggy was reduced to kindling, and as I stood there I found myself crying like a baby. I guess I was like some mules I have known ... it took a mighty wallop to get my attention ... but I have never forgotten the lesson I learned that night about misplaced values. Some folks never come to learn the difference between Pride and Dignity ... each one demands that you hold up your head, but whereas one can lift you over many a rough spot, the other can be counted on to bring you to your knees. I ended up on my knees that night of the early October snow and when I finally stood up, God and I had come to an understanding and we've remained good friends to this day.

Seven

I had a little growing up to do ... nothing like having a wife dependent on you to bring that fact home. Ellen and I got married on December second and I can't recall a colder winter before or since. Because of my foolishness with the buggy, I didn't have any money to spare for a wedding trip so Ellen had to make do with the promise of one to come in the by-and-by. As it turned out she didn't have to wait too long. Her sister, Nan, married and moved to Atlanta and Ellen cried so much, missing her favorite sister and best friend, that Mr.Wilson bought us train tickets to go visit them. My, we felt grand ... that is until the sights and sounds of that big Georgia town turned us back into country bumpkins as we walked around with our eyes and mouths open in awe of all the strange and wonderous things around us. But, you know, when we got back home Ellen declared that, proud as she was of Nan's set-up there in Atlanta, she was not in the least bit envious and I noticed she couldn't wait to get out of her traveling clothes and head out to see if the pear tree was in bloom.

Anyways, I was working in Mr.Gribble's store morning till night and saving every cent I could to buy a little farm that touched our property on the south that the owner had told me he needed to sell real bad. Ellen stayed busy that winter by sewing curtains and stuff and planning the garden she would put in come spring. I brought her a seed catalog and a Farmer's Almanac and by March she had figured out exactly when to plant her English peas, spring onions and radishes and as soon as the ground had warmed up enough to work, she had me out there turning over the dirt in perfectly lined up rows she had laid out with string and, with the seeds she had had Mr. Gribble order, she was ready to go. She also had me fence in a little bit of yard so she could keep a few Dominecker hens. Next came an old milk cow I was able to buy cheap from a family that was moving to town, so come summer we were eating like kings and still had enough left over to put up for rainy days and to share with our neighbors. That first year saw the start of a custom that was to continue for sixty-seven years. Every Sunday, just as I was settling down with my Bible or the newspaper, I'd hear, "Felix, come take this basket of eggs (or okra or tomatoes or biscuits and sorghum, or pat of butter) over to Mrs.Clark (or Mr.Grissom or old lady Fuston or that nice Mr.Ramsey) cause I hear she's down in her back (or has a fever or broke an ankle or lost his wife)" and off I'd go. She took a real delight in fixing the basket up real pretty with a checkered napkin or a bunch of violets or even a nest of reindeer moss she'd found in the woods, and I'd swell up with pride when someone would say what a fine woman I'd married.

One thing about Ellen's gardens ... there were always as many flowers as there were vegetables in those rows. She'd make out like the marigolds were to keep away the rabbits or some such excuse, but the truth of the matter was she just craved the sight and smell of sweet peas and pinks all mixed in with the runner beans and rhubarb. I don't remember seeing our kitchen table without a bunch of something or other on it ... even in months when nothing was in bloom in the garden there would be a bowl of red and yellow maple leaves or buckbush berries or just a group of funny shaped gourds. I've heard more than one person say that Ellen had a sense of what was pleasing to the eye and a style about her that other women aimed for all their lives and never got.

Well, our hard work and saving paid off and, after a few years went around the bend, we saw our small plot of land grow to ten acres and our family expand to include a baby girl, Katie Pearl. Right from the start you could tell she would grow up to be a heartbreaker. I was hoping for her mother's coloring but she ended up with mine ... dark hair and gray-blue eyes, but at least she got the curls. (It still pains me to remember the time, shortly after she married ... it was right after the war and all the young city girls seemed to go loco or something, shortening their skirts up to their knees and carrying on like white trash ... she came home to visit and when I saw she had cut off those beautiful long curls just so's to look like those fast living Nashville girls, I had to turn away so she wouldn't see my tears.)

As soon as Katie Pearl started toddling around she formed the habit of holding on to one of my legs to steady herself. It's a wonder I didn't develop the limp I'd escaped when I broke my leg, cause she kept up that way of hanging on whenever we went anywhere together, and even though I was a pretty long-legged fella, it finally got to be pretty embarassing, as well as uncomfortable, as she got older and her hand grabbed me further and further up! But there wasn't much that little gal could do to rile me. I thought she hung the moon and I was forever ready to help her find the stars if she as much as asked!

Is that you, Jacob? Sure you can have a piece of peppermint candy. Haven't seen you in a while. Thought maybe I'd talked your ear off last time you were here. How long have I lived here? Let's see ...

Eight

Katie Pearl says she can still remember her first trip in to town ... that would be McMinnville, our county seat, at that time still a small place as cities go, but big enough to be impressive to a little girl used to the likes of Dibrell! Maybe she only remembers hearing me tell about that day, cause I still chuckle thinking about her reaction to the crowds and their reaction to her.

I think I told you that Ellen's daddy traded livestock for a living ... well, for every occasion coming along that called for a parade, Mr. Wilson couldn't wait to volunteer his horses, if for nothing but the chance to advertise the merchandise, and he usually insisted that his big black stallion, Beau, be in the lead. When the new century turned over, the Warren County city fathers decided a celebration was in order and what better way to kick off festivities than a parade, followed by fireworks and speeches on the square. Now, Ellen had been riding since she could balance herself on the back of a horse and Beau was always one of her favorite mounts, so when her Pa asked her if she wanted to be the one to ride him in the parade it didn't take her two seconds to say "yes."

Mrs. Wilson had sent to Atlanta for a black habit and boots for Ellen and Mr. Wilson had had a red leather bridle specially made for Beau. I'm sure you can conjure up the picture they made ... Ellen with her flaming red hair set off by the black habit and shiny boots, side-saddle on that high stepping, high spirited, coal black horse, held in check by her little gloved hands on the red leather reins. The crowd liked to have gone crazy! They cheered and clapped and the more they roared the more Beau pranced and Ellen sat there like a queen going to her coronation. Katie Pearl was sitting on my shoulders, high above the crowd along Main Street, taking it all in and not missing a trick. So when she spied her mother coming, the object of everyone's attention, she grabbed hold of my suspenders, and bucking up and down on my back, hollered out, "Look everbody, I can ride good as my mama!" Ellen heard her and laid her head back and laughed out loud and every man, woman and child within earshot turned round and smiled at that pretty, curly headed girl sitting there atop a very red-faced Felix Badger. When, several years later, we moved to McMinnville, real often someone would remind me of that scene and invariably the comment would be accompanied by a big grin!

On one of my trips in to town I made the acquaintance of a Mr. B.D. Moore. He asked me if I wasn't the "horse" that little gal rode in the New Century parade and when I owned up to being one and the same we sorta took off from there and a mutually pleasing relationship developed. One day I looked up from putting together an order for Miss Annie Womack and saw B.D. coming through the door of Mr.Gribble's store. After we shook and howdy-ed, he said, "Felix, how would you feel about going into business with me?" It seemed he'd been mulling over the idea of opening a wholesale grocery business and needed a partner who knew something about merchandising. Well, I told him if there was anything I'd had experience in it was selling people what they wanted to buy ... whether they knew they wanted to buy it or not!

I must admit the idea had a lot of appeal to me. For some time I'd been thinking that there wasn't much opportunity to better myself in Dibrell, and I'd been mightily impressed with the prosperity I'd witnessed in town, so I told him I'd give it some thought ... meaning, I'd see if Ellen was as taken with the idea as I was.

My timing was pretty bad though, cause when I busted in the house, all wild-eyed and talking a mile a minute about B.D.'s offer, she was in the midst of brewing up a batch of herb tea to try and comfort a baby screaming with the colic, and her disposition, as well as his, left a bit to be desired!

You see, a few months earlier Ellen had delivered a fine little boy that we named Ransom Alberto for his two grandfathers. She had miscarried a couple of times after Katie Pearl was born so this birth was a source of joy to both of us. Those red-hair genes finally came through and it seemed that Berto's arrival fulfilled all our hopes and dreams for an ideal family. But, coming as it did in the midst of her frustration and worry, my enthusiasm for the new venture wasn't exactly contagious! She didn't quite put her pretty little foot smack down but the look she gave me, plus her lack of any other response, let me know that she wasn't wildly excited about the prospect.

I decided my best move at that point was to get myself out of the house so I went over to talk to Mr.Wilson. He was a smart business man and I set great store by his advice. I'll never forget what he said that day. "Felix, when women become mothers they just naturally make nests for their chicks and it's like pulling teeth to shoo them off to a new roost ... but you're the provider so you need to go and do what you gotta do and I'll back you all the way."

He not only backed me up but he went with me to Mr.Rawlings' bank in McMinnville and, with the understanding that Ellen's name be listed on the title deed, he co-signed my note. So that's how "Moore and Badger, Wholesale Grocers, Dealers in Furs, Feed and Seed" came to be.

It didn't take too long to sell the place on the Sparta road or to help Mr.Gribble train the young Magness boy to take my place. It took a bit longer to find the house on College Street in McMinnville but when I did, it made Ellen forget she was ever lukewarm about moving to town. And that note I signed ... it was paid off in full in only two years, and Mr.Rawlings never again mentioned the need for a co-signer when I needed money for other business deals. "Your own 'John Henry' is enough for me, Felix," he'd say and to this day he's never had cause to regret this decision.

Nine

We were going through the "dog days" of summer when one day a fella from out near Faulkner's Springs came in talking about how much cooler it was out at his place than in town. Now I was working pretty hard through this gap. You see, B.D. was what you call a "silent partner" ... however there were times he'd come by with so many suggestions as to how things should be done, I found myself wishing he would be a bit more "silent" ... and I had sensed that Ellen was getting a little testy, what with keeping a tight rein on an active toddler as well as a growing girl who was more hindrance than help around the house and a husband too tired at night to sympathize. So I went home that evening and after Ellen came down from putting Berto to bed, I mentioned that conversation I'd had with the man from the country and asked if she'd like to pack a picnic lunch and drive out there Sunday after church. Kate got so excited about the plan that Ellen caught the fever and the following day our house was filled with good smells and happy talk and you'd have thought we were going on a trip across the ocean instead of five miles out in the country!

Well, Sunday came and even though it was a bit cloudy we packed up the buggy (I had replaced Felix's Folly with one that was much more sedate and sensible) with baskets of fried chicken, dressed eggs, sausage biscuits, pound cake, and lemonade, with blankets to sit on and yellow sulfa to ward off chiggers, and after moving things around till we had room for people, we set out. It took us almost an hour to make the trek but everyone was in such a good mood that the time passed most pleasantly and when we rounded the last bend and started down the hill into the valley where the creek ran we could actually feel the air getting cooler ... course it didn't dawn on us that that was partly due to the fact that the sun had disappeared behind a very ugly looking black cloud! We found a perfect little clearing among the trees near the water, where the kids could wade, Ellen could gather ferns for her garden, and I could stretch out for a nap, but scarcely had we spread the blanket and got out the baskets when there came a loud clap of thunder and drops of rain that would fill a thimble began to fall. Just down the creek aways I had noticed the water wheel of a grist mill turning, so we grabbed the food and made a bee line for shelter.

There was a man inside sacking corn meal and he 'lowed as how it was no skin off his nose if we had our picnic there out of the weather, and after we noticed his longing glances at Ellen's chicken we asked him to join us. While we waited for the shower to pass over I got to talking to the miller about the operation there and found out that the man who owned the mill was getting old and might soon be shutting it down. Well, the wheels inside my head started turning faster than the mill wheel outside. At Moore and Badger we had been buying our bulk meal from a place much like this one over in Woodbury and it seemed like it would serve two purposes if I was to own this place ... The store would have a closer source for its meal and my pockets could be filled with the money that was now going into some other fella's purse.

I pushed this thought to the back of my mind for the time being. The sky cleared. We went back to the creek bank and while Kate was turning over rocks to point out the crawfish to Berto, I helped Ellen dig the ferns that turned loose their hold on their resting place much easier now that the rain had relaxed the soil. That night all of us fell asleep with dirt under our fingernails and smiles on our faces.

The next day, as soon as there came a lull at the store, I turned the key in the big roll-top desk that sat just inside the front door, pulled down the shade and hurried around the corner to see Mr.Rawlings. Seems he was familiar with Mr.Faulkner's mill as well as with that gentleman's age and physical condition, and when he heard my plan for taking advantage of this two-sided opportunity, he cleared the way for my loan to go through once I had come to reasonable terms with the owner. He asked if he might have a share in the venture, but I sensed he was halfway pulling my leg, so I smiled and told him I'd just furnish him with all the meal he needed for the hoe cakes Mrs. Rawlings was famous for.

The ending to this story came several weeks later. I met with Mr.Faulkner and we took to each other right off. He said, "Felix, I remember calling your Pa once when a bad tooth had me climbing the walls and it looks like you are fixing to relieve me of something that has become as worrisome to me at this time as that tooth was to me then!" So with one stroke of a pen I found myself the owner of a grist mill as well as the best picnic spot this side of Ben Loman Mountain.

My goodness, Jacob. You're all grown up. Next thing we know you'll be tall as me. What are you doing with that pencil and tablet? School assignment? No, I don't mind. You know how I like to talk! What you want to hear about?

Ten

I swear I believe Warren County has more cyclone touchdowns than any place this side of Kansas. Everybody has his own tall tale to add when the subject comes up around here. Ellen likes to tell about a friend if hers who saw a funnel coming across the fields one day ... she ran to the foot of the stairs and yelled, "Hurry, children. Get to the cellar," and they all tumbled down the steps just in time to escape the storm that demolished their house. Ellen says if she did that, that Kate would want to finish dressing her doll and Berto would want to know "how come?" and before you knew it they would all be scattered in pieces over the fields along with the bricks and boards!

A few years after we moved to town I heard about a little farm for sale out near Centertown and as I had been feeling the need for space and growing room as well as a place to keep a few cows and pigs, I made a deal with the owner. The farm had two families living on it, one colored and one white, and both Mr. Adams and "Odie" Beech agreed to stay on and help with the farm chores in return for the deed to a couple of acres each. "Odie" had a girl named "Sallie" who said she would come in town to do the washing and ironing and help Ellen run after Berto. Mrs. Wilson had recently died and I knew that having some time to get away from home and

41

visit with lady friends would perk up Ellen's spirits but, as it turned out, Sallie was so good-natured and full of conversation that Ellen had a good time just staying home and working alongside her.

Sallie came in one morning after a specially bad storm and her eyes were almost popping out of her head. "Miss Ellen, that cyclone done come right through the farm last night and turned Mr. Adam's house plum inside out!" We had a good laugh over her wild and colorful description but sure enough, when I rode out later in the day I looked up on the rise where the Adams' house stood and realized I was looking at the back door instead of the front! The winds had been strong enough to pick up that little frame house, turn it back to front, and set it back, neat as you please, on the foundation.

Now the Adamses had a passel of chillun and one of them was a boy who was a bit simple minded. Junior was about twenty-five years old and must have weighed close to three hundred pounds, but his brain never made it pass the first grade. All the little neighbor children were scared to death of him cause when he would come running to join in whatever game they were playing, just the sight of that big grown man running at them and whooping like a banshee was enough to send them high-tailing it to their mama's skirts.

Well, when I knocked on the front door, which was now sitting three feet above the level of the back yard, here came Mrs. Adams, followed by Junior, who was covered with more bruises and cuts than some cur dog who'd been bested by a bobcat. When I asked what in the world had happened she said, "You know, we had one of them hurry-canes come through here last night and what with the house turning around and all, Junior got sick to his stomick and when he opened the back door to head to the privy, he run smack into the front porch! Poor thang were so addled by it all, he plum forgot about throwing up," and she went on to say, "Mr. Adams and I have 'bout decided to leave the house setting like it be. We're afraid if Junior finds the privy done moved agin, he'll be stopped up for life."

Eleven

It wasn't exactly every day that a lady came in to do business at Moore and Badger, so I was taken a bit by surprise the day I looked up and saw Miss Effie Hillis, all dressed up fit to kill, coming through the door. Now Miss Effie had remained a spinster for all those many years cause she was so shy she turned three shades of red if a fella as much as spoke to her, so I knew she wasn't there to pass the time of day, and it was too late in the season for her to be needing onion sets. As I got up and went round to speak to her the only things running through my mind were that Berto had been teasing her big yellow cat again or that her mother (who must be all of a hundred by now) had passed and she wanted to enlist my help in carrying the casket at the funeral. But I was wrong on both counts. Seems Miss Effie wanted to rent the empty space up over the store and set up her piano to give lessons to all the boys and girls in town whose folks were convinced that their youngster was the next famous vaudeville star. Her old mother needed peace and quiet at home ever bit as much as Miss Effie needed the money her teaching would bring in, so since that space was just sitting there going begging, I told her she was welcome to try and bring a little culture to McMinnville and all the rent I asked was that she number Kate among her pupils.

I never stood taller in my little girl's eyes than I did that night when I came home and sprung this bit of news. It was rare enough to coax a smile from her in those days as she was going through that period when girls get sassy and boys get sullen, but when I asked her if she was interested in taking advantage of this opportunity, she actually jumped up and down, hugged me around the neck, and ran next door to tell Sophie Anderson, her best friend that week, about her good fortune.

It was summer and school wasn't in session and that second story must have been 120 degrees but from the day the draymen unloaded the piano and muscled it up the outside stairs, Kate haunted the place. Opening the windows cooled it off a bit but her enthusiasm only heated up all the more. She was like Paul Revere, spreading the news, and I'm sure she was responsible for enrolling at least half of Miss Effie's students.

What with her running up and down the steps and popping in for peanuts, I saw more of my daughter that year than I had in some time. I was busy patting myself on the back for finding the way to make everyone happy, when one day as I was closing up here came Miss Effie with a most serious look on her face.

"Felix, I'm afraid we're just wasting everyone's time trying to teach Kate to read music."

"But, Miss Effie", I said, "I thought you told Ellen that Kate had a real talent."

"I did say she was talented," she said, "but she'll never learn to read sheet music as long as she can pick out any tune she hears without so much as a written note in front of her."

Miss Effie was puzzled, to say the least, when I busted out laughing. Had she but known it was from pure relief that her dour expression had been caused by something with such a simple solution. A few weeks later, Kate and I rode the train to Nashville and picked out a piano for her to play at home. It crowded the parlor a bit but the toe-tapping tunes she played and the hymn singing she accompanied gave us all a lot of pleasure and Miss Effie never understood why I thanked HER in return each time she thanked ME for the use of that old hot attic.

❦ ❦ ❦ ❦

As I am called on to think back, a couple of things related to Kate's piano playing come to mind. First off, a few years later when ballroom dancing captured all the young folks fancy, Kate sweet talked her brother into helping her and they gave lessons to all her friends who wanted to learn how to do the "Bunny Hop" and all those dances they were doing out at Faulkner's Springs Hotel on Saturday nights. Miss Effie's lessons had come to an end with her death and I gave in to Kate's begging to use the space over the store for these sessions. I've got to say I laughed to myself at the notion of that dirty faced, silly little red headed boy squiring some dainty young lady around the dance floor, but it turned out that Berto had so much rhythm that before you knew it he had taken over all the teaching while Kate just played the tunes he called out to her.

As luck would have it, the next time his musical abilities showed up was when he was talked into playing the drums while in the marching band at Columbia Military Academy, and as you can imagine, Ellen and I were hard-pressed to muster up any enthusiasm for this newly discovered aptitude!

I mentioned Faulkner's Springs Hotel ... well, this fine structure had been built to cater to families from Nashville who could afford to escape from the city's summertime heat spells and had proved to be a real going concern. Mr. Anderson, Sophie's father, ran the establishment and was a friend of mine and as he knew that Kate played the piano with some measure of skill, he prevailed on her to come out occasionally and play for the guests to dance. Among the regular patrons was the Warner family whose three handsome sons created quite a stir in the female circles around town. At one time or another, Kate "stepped out with" all three boys but it was Will who captured her heart.

After the war, when Will came around with serious courting on his mind, Kate naturally assumed it was at least partially because of her musical talent that she had caught the eye of this attractive visitor from the city. But one night when she left him swinging on the porch and went inside to sit down at the piano and perform a most ambitious rendition of "When You Wore A Tulip", he appeared at the door and announced, "Kate, I don't know one note from another, and if you're playing that thing for my benefit, you're wasting your time."

Well, obviously she forgave him for what must have been most crushing blow to her pride, cause they were married and lived together happily for many years, but I just know there was a scar there that never quite healed cause, other than at church, I never again heard her play ... and I, for one, sure did miss it.

Twelve

Ellen's people are more prolific than mine. I swear she must have kinfolk in just about every county in Tennessee. Once we actually counted up to twenty-five first cousins and it seemed like she would find some reason to go gallivanting off to visit one or tother of them every few months. She used to take Berto along till the time he put his foot down and declared he was tired of being nice to prissy girls and sissy boys, most of them being younger and no fun at all to go fishing with.

It must have been while Ellen was away on one of these visits, cause I remember being left to look after Berto, that I got word from the mine that there had been some trouble. Oh, I didn't tell you about owning a coal mine? Well, it seems that once it became legal for the state to lease out convicts to work in the mines, everybody and his brother jumped on the bandwagon. Now, as I had never been one to pass up an opportunity to better myself financially, nothing would do but I buy myself a piece of Harrison Ferry Mountain and start hauling out the coal.

On this particular day my foreman, Bob Slatten, sent a young fella riding lickity-split down the mountain to tell me there had been an accident and that I had to come right away.

So I hollered for Berto, grabbed Ma's old snakebite remedy (the one she used to have me go gather the fall asters for) and off we went. That mountain was the choice homesite for the biggest timber rattlers this side of the Mississippi River and I assumed the emergency must have come when one of the guys stepped into the underbrush to relieve himself and met up with one of these varmints. A similar encounter had taken place the week before and was fresh on my mind.

But, as it turned out, I was way off base. When we got there I discovered a much more serious situation. One of the mine cars that was used to bring out the coal had broken down, and in spite of Bob Slatten's warnings, one of the men got underneath to try and discover what the trouble was, and the car started up again and rolled over his arm and cut it off clean as a whistle. When we heard this I saw Berto's eyes get big as saucers and ever bit of color leave his face. Ever since he was a little boy he couldn't see blood without getting woozie, so I decided right then to get him away from there as quick as possible. We had two old mules around to carry equipment back and forth so I told Bob's sixteen year old son, who happened to be there helping his dad that day, to put Berto on one and for the two of them to head on home.

We made the poor man who'd lost his arm as comfortable as possible with a little whiskey someone had hidden in a hollow tree and, after staunching the flow of blood as best we could, we put him in the wagon bed on some blankets and headed for town and Dr. Mulligan as fast as we could with him moaning and the two of us praying all the way.

When I finally got home that evening I saw that Ellen had gotten back from Gallatin and was standing on the front porch with tears streaming down her face. I started in to comforting her by telling what Dr. Mulligan had said and assuring her it was a miracle the man hadn't died from shock, but she cut me off in mid-sentence.

"Felix Badger," (well, I knew right then I was in for some sort of unpleasantness) "I go off for two days and leave my baby in your care and what do I find when I get back ... the poor child will be scarred for life and all you can think of is some convict who probably killed someone to end up where he was anyway."

I've never understood how a woman's logic progresses from point A to point B, but I'd lived with this one long enough to know I'd best go easy till I got to the root of her distress so I stood there and held my tongue while she finished. When I pieced it all together I learned that the boy who'd brought Berto down the mountain only had one horse blanket, which he naturally kept for his own comfort, and those mules were so skinny their backbones stuck out like ridgepoles. By the time they'd covered the eight or ten miles between here and there the little fella's bottom was raw and bleeding, he and his mother were in tears and I was in the doghouse, sure nuff!

I vowed right then that I would never again use another man's wretched state to make myself better off, and so as to divest myself of some of those tainted dollars, I bought a bell for Pa's old church at Mt. Pisgah and surprised Brother Ramsey with a specially generous donation next time the plate was passed at the Presbyterian Church in town.

Now Berto ... he emerged from the experience with some scars allright but it also provided him with fodder for one of his favorite stories. One that never failed to bring laughs from whichever audience he happened to be entertaining at the moment was about how he got HIS war wounds in the Battle of the Asses on Harrison Ferry Mountain!

Come in, Jacob. What are you doing, coming to the front door? You drove here? In a car? You know, I can remember when the first automobiles were built ...

Thirteen

The first picture I saw of Henry Ford and his Model T really captured my interest and from then on I read every thing I could about these new machines, and Kate was as smitten as I was ... however, in her case, I think she was mainly taken with those long flowing coats and veils the ladies wore riding about the countryside. Anyway, we got the fever and made our plans to go to Nashville to look into the possibility of buying an automobile. Berto was too busy playing baseball to be interested and Ellen didn't want to go with us cause "nothing on God's green earth would get her in one of those contraptions", so Kate and I set out on our own.

We picked out a little Ford roadster and the salesman sent along a young man to drive us home and to stay long enough to teach us the fundamentals of driving. The roads weren't much to brag about back then and Woodbury Hill about bested both the car and the driver. But he finally discovered that the reverse gear was powerful enough to get us up that steep grade, and after stopping to repair several punctures and once to let a dairy herd cross the road to their barn, we made it home ... as I remember it took us about seven hours.

Ours wasn't the first car in town but I'm sure it was the busiest! Kate took to driving like she'd been born with wheels and I noticed that after a little bit Ellen found all kinds of excuses to need a ride to the market, or over to Beulah's for a card game, or to carry a jar of boiled custard to cousin Belle who was laid up with her latest misery. Soon we began to wonder how we ever got along without that little Ford.

A few years later another automobile was to change our lives…and in a most dreadful way. We sent Kate to "finish" her education at Belmont College in Nashville. (In order to make her mother feel better about the separation I arranged with the two ladies who ran the school for Kate to be allowed to come home any time she chose and I gave her a railroad pass to make this possible.) While she was there she made friends with a girl from Georgia named Sappho Pickering and the two of them had a fine old time visiting back and forth. One Sunday afternoon they were out driving in the Buckhead area of Atlanta with a young man who wanted to show off his new Premier runabout and, rounding a curve on Rosswell Road, they had a blowout and, because he was traveling at a high rate of speed, he lost control. The car turned over twice and crashed into a big pine tree on the side of the road.

The telegram Dr.Pickering sent us from Grady Hospital only said that Kate had broken her leg and remembering my own experience I had no reason to expect the nightmare I encountered when I arrived in Atlanta. It seems they had had an awful time removing Kate from the wreckage and when they did they found the large thigh bone broken and protruding through the skin and she was bleeding profusely from the wound. When I first saw her they had set the leg and had it in a cast from hip to ankle and her face was the color of ashes. I understood from the doctors that they were very concerned about her loss of blood.

As soon as she was able to recognize me her face lit up and she made some joke about always knowing that boy had more dollars than sense, and I knew then that her natural "spunk" would carry her through anything that lay ahead. I wired Ellen assuring her that Kate was going to be fine and then I sent round to Maier and Berkele for them to bring over a tray of diamond brooches for her to choose from. The dainty crescent moon she pointed to we pinned on her nightgown then and there, and to this day I never see a new moon without repeating the prayer of thanks I whispered to God that day when they showed me what was left of the automobile the young folks had been riding in and I realized what a narrow escape my little girl had had.

But that was not the end of it. For six months she could do nothing but lie around entertaining her friends while Ellen and Sallie waited on her hand and foot till finally the day came when we returned to Grady to have her leg freed from the burdensome cast. You can imagine how crushed we were when the grim faced doctor stood there and told us the bone had healed incorrectly and would have to be rebroken and set.

So that meant another endless six months of recovering and this time we were much more apprehensive as we headed back to Atlanta to have the cast removed. Fortunately they found the healing to be acceptable but it was also apparent that Kate would be left with her right leg considerably shorter than the other. I suppose it was vanity (or pride, that same old Badger bug-a-boo) but she never wanted anyone to know about this imperfection and in time she found a shoe man who would alter all her slippers so that the average person was never aware of her slight limp. However her days of romping and running were over and as she got older her mother and I would catch her turning her head to hide the pain as her leg reacted to the arthritis that made its home there.

My love affair with automobiles was indeed over and I guess you might say that after Kate's accident, I looked on them as my "enemies," and to this day there are those who maintain I use my own car as a weapon, pointing it vengefully at any other vehicle in my path ... but you don't believe that, now do you?

Fourteen

When the First World War exploded in Europe it wasn't really a surprise 'cause we'd been reading all about the fussing and feuding over there for some time but here in Warren County its effect was chiefly felt when the price of sugar went sky high causing everybody and his brother to rush out and plant sorghum.

In the Badger household the war became personal when Will Warner, who was flying airplanes for the army, would come calling on Kate whenever he was home on furlough. I've got to tell you, just the sight of those shiny black aviator boots was enough to send the local ladies into a tizzy of bandage rolling and scarf knitting, the likes of which you've never seen! And that was when Berto was off at military school. Whenever he came home, decked out in HIS fancy uniform, Ellen would cry herself to sleep cause she was convinced he would end up in the army and get himself shot or drowned in one of those French rivers the papers kept writing about.

What we knew about the war we read in the newspapers cause radios hadn't made their appearance in McMinnville. However, they weren't really vital to the spread of information as long as I kept the gunnysack by the stove filled with peanuts and as long as Will Hillis and Nat Higgenbottom kept their knives good and sharp! When the news came in about Alvin York's one man battle with the Huns the reaction was nothing compared to the excitement stirred up by the heroism of our own neighbor, Brown Cunningham. When the stories of his exploits hit the papers, the peanut hulls and cedar shavings had to be swept up three times a day instead of just onest!

That crowd around the stove was made up of pert near the same faces day in and day out (except when an occasional drummer would stop by to spice up the conversation with a story or two) and everybody got along just fine, being tolerant of one another's fits and failures, except for one fella who not only hogged the talking space but ruffled feathers with his know-it-all manner. His name was Fuller Washington, but everyone called him, "Fuller Beans" because of his habit of bragging as well as another habit that caused his proximity to be most un-pleasant, but you know, he never caught on as to why his chair was always being pushed back and away from the rest of the circle.

Now Berto was born with a bit of the devil in him and when he heard some of us talking about old Fuller one day, he cooked up a joke that folks around here still chuckle about. I had a broken-down pie safe in the rear of the store that I used to keep nail kegs and onion sets in. Berto tore off a piece of tin from the side of that safe and used it to make a seat for one of the chairs whose caning had broken through. Then he carefully wired a candle between the chair legs. I guess you're ahead of me, right? Well, the next day when Fuller came in that chair was the only one empty and after he sat down, Berto slipped around behind, leaned over and lit the candle. The whole group busted out laughing just as Fuller was finishing up one of his long-winded tales and I imagine he thought his wit was finally being appreciated, but just then the heat took hold of that tin chair bottom and the poor man let out a howl the likes of which hadn't been heard around here since the spanking Livia Smoot gave little Teddy the day he grabbed her Sunday corset off the line to use as a battle flag in a game of king-on-the-mountain.

As you can imagine, it was hard for me to keep a straight face when I fussed at Berto for getting laughs at another man's expense, especially in the midst of the loud guffaws coming from the others, but in reality we were all in his debt. It was several weeks before Fuller joined the circle again and, when he did, he wasn't nearly so cocky ... though the fellas still jockeyed for seats so as not to have to sit next to old "Beans"!

Now why on earth would that silly incident come to my mind when I try and recollect the war that was to "make the world safe for democracy," as President Wilson said? Maybe the connection is that you should never take your security for granted ... whether you're Fuller Washington or Washington,D.C., you need to be wary of the circle you sit in!

Fifteen

The most admirable man I ever met? That would have to be Mr. Cordell Hull. It was my honor and privilege to be in his company once when I was called on to go over to Sparta to try and collect from a guy who had reneged on a debt. I was advised to see a lawyer named Hudson (who turned out to be the brother of the "Doc Hudson" Pa had ridden out with!). When I went to his office, who was there but Mr. Hull himself, and he had a group around him hanging on his every word. I was about to excuse myself when Mr. Hudson said, "Sit down, young man. You might just learn something that will stand you in good stead down the road."

Well, I didn't exactly add to my store of knowledge that day except to discover what a natural-born story teller Mr. Hull was. He told about piloting rafts of logs a hundred feet long downriver from his home in Byrdstown to Nashville when he was still a youngster, and then he went on to recount some of his experiences fighting in the war with Spain. At the time I met him, he had already served as circuit court judge and he was soon persuaded to recall some of his more colorful cases. He said that legal ethics prevented him from discussing court proceedings but he did tell us about the time his best friend came before him on the charge of carving his name on a public building. Everyone expected him to let the fella off but Judge Hull fined him fifty dollars ... which shocked the courtroom as well as the culprit, who sheepishly handed over his check. After court adjourned, the judge sought out his friend and gave him fifty dollars from his own pocket and a pat on the back to reinstitute the friendship.

I don't remember whether or not I collected on my note that day, but I do remember vividly the impression the future Secretary of State made on me. From that day on I followed his career in the newspapers with a new interest. I didn't live in his district and was never in a position to vote for him when he ran for congressman, however I enthusiastically supported and voted for him in his Senate race.

His successor on the bench said that "Cordell Hull never starts anywhere less he knows where he's going and" once he sets out "he never turns back". I was to think about this when, several years later, Mr.Rawlings approached me and said that the local politicians were looking for a good Democrat, who had both farming and business interests at heart, to run for mayor in the next election. He seemed to think I filled the bill and I went home that night as excited as a kid on Christmas Eve.

I couldn't wait to talk it over with Ellen but she punctured my balloon in a hurry. "Pshaw! What do you know about running a city? Leave it to them that's been doing it all their lives." Well, that kinda got my dander up. I could almost hear Mr.Hull saying something like "If honest men don't take on jobs of responsibility, believe you me the crooks will be there waiting to step in and do things their way."

The next morning I took myself down to the courthouse and filed all the necessary papers to enter the race and from then till election day I put all my energies into rounding up votes. The stove in the back of the store provided my platform and when the heat of summer drove the whittlers out to the benches on the square, I followed along and told anyone who'd listen about my plans for helping our town survive its growing pains.

Finally the big day dawned and while I was hanging around the square trying to look important and sway as many last minute votes as possible, I looked up and here came Ellen out of the courthouse, straightening her hat and pulling on her gloves. You could have knocked me over with a feather cause she had never showed any interest whatsoever in political goings-on even though ladies had been allowed to vote for several years. I told her I was sure glad she had come around to my way of thinking cause I would need her support if I became mayor. She looked at me with those brown eyes dancing and said, "Felix, this is the biggest fool thing you've ever done! I came down here to vote AGAINST you."

Well, in spite of her I got elected and I suppose I was a pretty fair-to-middling mayor. I may not have filled many pages in the history books, but I did keep Junior Adams out of jail the time that silly Odele Stubblefield said he was trying to "have his way with her" when he only wanted to hug her like he'd seen Odele's pa do the day before. And I did get a volunteer fire department started after the man who had the farm next to mine out on the road to Centertown stood and watched his barn and three milk cows burn up cause he had a bad back and couldn't round up any of his neighbors to come and help.

The whole experience taught me that I would certainly never be a congressman or senator but I did cultivate an interest in the workings of government that stayed with me all the rest of my life and after all, I did get Ellen to the polls ... once!

What're you grinning so big about, Jacob? You're gonna get married? I can't believe you're old enough for that. Seems like yesterday my daughter, Kate, got married and she's heaps older than you!

Sixteen

The new Singer Sewing Machine I bought for Ellen was pert near worn out six months after it was delivered. You see, Will had given Kate a ring and when the first wave of excitement died down Ellen and Kate lit into planning Kate's trousseau like they were demon possessed! At first they just pored over the ladies' books hour after hour and next here came the packages from Nashville and Atlanta ... bolt after bolt of ribbon, lace, and cloth the likes of which would surely have given some Main Street merchant enough goods to open a new store. 'Fore long we acquired a sort of semi-permanent house guest ... Millie Maud Morroney, a seamstress that Ellen swore knew more about things like tucks and gores and fluting than anyone for miles around, became a regular fixture in our house on College Street. Got so a body had to plan his route getting from the kitchen to the front porch what with patterns and pictures and half finished costumes lying around everywhere you wanted to step. I found myself staying later than was hardly necessary at the store cause I didn't seem to be needed for anything at home but signing checks.

When the new wardrobe trunk came it appeared they spent more time "gussying" it up, lining it with some sort of pink silky stuff and sticking ribbons and rosebuds in every available corner, than they did on filling up the drawers.

'Course that was just the beginning. Soon here came the traveling suits, the morning dresses, church dresses, and party gowns ... boots, slippers, and something called "mules" ... big hats, little hats, and of course all those undergarments with such lace and ribbons swirling around that getting into (or out of) them must have been quite complicated. Even old Felix came in for a few oohs and ahs and hugs the day I came home with three really fine beaver pelts a fella had brought in to trade, and 'fore you could say "Jack Robinson" Millie Maud had fashioned a sort of long vest with pockets for Kate to wear over a kinda plain brown skirt and blouse and I must say she looked like some sort of fine young lady sure nuff when she put it on to model for us. I guess that was the first time it came to me that my little girl was really going to marry and leave home.

Now, Will Warner was a calm and patient man but, like most calm and patient men, he had his "fill up and spill over" point. One late summer Sunday we were packing up after we had all been picnicing at Faulkner's Springs, and, looking over at the little waterfall there, he said, "Kate, you say you would give anything to go to Niagara Falls on your honeymoon ... well, I guess we better be getting on up there before it freezes over," and the next thing I knew we were sitting in the front pew of the church, watching Katie Pearl walk down the aisle to marry Will.

I worked it out for Berto and John, the handyman who worked for us, to cart Kate's trunk over to the Union Station in Nashville where the honeymooners were to board the train after spending the night at the Hermitage Hotel. That morning, when Berto jumped up onto the seat of the truck, he disturbed an old hat of John's which had been taken over by a mama field mouse as a cozy warm nest to house her newborns. John proceeded to deposit mama and babies on the ground but Berto begged him to let one tiny vole come along for the ride to Nashville and John, knowing he'd never wear that hat again anyway, said all right.

Now at sixteen, Berto still hadn't outgrown his boyish devilment (as a matter of fact,I don't suppose he ever did) and somewhere between Woodbury and Murfreesboro he remembered that soft, furry vest in his sister's wardrobe. When John stopped for gas, Berto climbed up on the truck bed, opened the trunk, and, seeing the vest hanging there in plain view, deposited the mouse in the conveniently accessible pocket. The little fella hunkered happily down, convinced he had returned to his mother's womb and the truck continued on its way to the station.

Naturally, Ellen and I knew nothing of all this carrying on till Kate and Will got back to Tennessee but we did puzzle a bit over the telegram from them which, in addition to the "thanks for everything" and the "this place is all we expected," was a PS saying, "Berto had better not be anywhere around when we next get to McMinnville!"

❦ ❦ ❦ ❦

Not too long ago, Kate, Ellen and I were laughing about all the fuss that was made over that trousseau and Kate said that her Ellen had packed that old trunk and carried it off to college in Virginia and when they got it down and opened it up there were still pieces of faded ribbon and pink silk roses in some of the drawers ... but no mouse, thank goodness!

Seventeen

"I didn't expect you to bring them here in litters." When Ellen came out with that the first time she saw Kate after the twins were born dead, I couldn't believe my ears. But when I saw the mournful expression on Kate's face relax into something that might even be called a smile and saw her pat her mama on the arm I realized that the two of them communicated in a way that others would never comprehend. You see, when Ellen was really scared, her first impulse was to lash out in anger and when Dr. Grizzard came to tell us that our eagerly awaited grandchild was not to be the tears poured down my cheeks and Ellen got mad, and in her frustration she hit out at whatever was handy. It was like the time I fell down the cellar steps with my arms full of Mason jars I had gone to fetch for Ellen's blackberry preserves. I musta made an awful racket and when she found me at the foot of the stairs I was out cold and was covered with blood where the jars had broke and cut my head and you know how even a little scratch on the head will bleed like crazy. Well, when I came to and we washed the blood off and she realized I wasn't dead or maimed or anything, Ellen lit in to fussing. "I don't know why you had to try and carry all those jars in one trip." and then she said "You made me go and burn my preserves!" ... why, you'd have thought I fell on purpose just to aggravate her!

So you see, when Ellen was afraid she might lose Kate as well as the grandbabies, her reaction was in character. You know, parents get so used to patching and soothing and making things right for their children that when something comes along that they can't fix, the feeling of frustration can be devastating.

But time is a great healer and with The Lord's help we were able to move on with our lives and a few years later Kate delivered a perfectly healthy, beautiful little boy. Billy came into the world smiling and hasn't stopped smiling to this day.

He came along so quick, we didn't have time to drive to Nashville. Will phoned early one hot August morning and I rushed to the back porch to call to Ellen just as she was coming through the grape arbor with her apron full of new-laid eggs and when I told her the news she dropped the corners of her apron, not even noticing that the still warm eggs were breaking around her feet, threw up her arms and hollered "Glory be !", and always after that, just the mention of his name would brighten her whole face

❦ ❦ ❦ ❦

Now Berto met Bess Erwin while he was in school in Columbia and had never gotten her out of his mind ... we didn't have to be too awfully smart to sense this cause he used every excuse under the sun to to head over that way whenever there was a baseball game or a dance in those parts and sure enough he persuaded that attractive young belle to marry him and we were able to welcome her into our home on College Street. Man, that gal could do it all ... she could sew as well as any professional seamstress I ever saw and when Ellen turned her loose in the kitchen the results were first-rate! She could fix anything from a leaky faucet to a broken window pane and we soon found ourselves calling for Bess whenever anything went wrong around the house.

Later when we found out that Bess and Berto were going to have a baby, I realized that if the two families were going to live under one roof then that roof needed to be bigger than the one we had. So one day I put Ellen in the car and we drove out to the end of Main Street to look at some property that was for sale. I'll never forget ... it was in late October and as we drove up the drive to the house we were surrounded by the red, yellow, and orange sugar maples that still put on a show each fall.

The old stone house that sat on the hill wasn't much to look at but Ellen's concerns went beyond that. As we walked out behind the house, she leaned over and grabbed a handful of dirt and squeezed it, looked up at the sun,and pronounced it a perfect garden spot. That sealed it ... we had found our home!

Our second grandchild was born in this house. Bess and Berto named her "Ann" and she was a honey. It was pure joy to see her grow day by day and to get to know her in a way we'd never know our Nashville grandchildren. Oh, I almost forgot ... soon after Ann was born, Kate and Will had a little girl, and they named her Ellen Wilson .... Boy, did that give her a lot to live up to!

Eighteen

Kate let Billy and Ellen spend some time with us each summer after they were old enough to do without a nurse. And since Ellen and Ann had each other to play with, Billy usually was allowed to bring along his friend, Bill, and after a few summers we treated him just like he was ours. He didn't escape Berto's teasing or Ellen's fussing when they got into mischief. Like the time the boys decided to make a pinball machine and the only piece of wood in the garage wide enough was the leaf to the cherry dining room table. I'll wager they had driven in a hundred and fifty tenpenny nails before Ellen went out to see what was keeping them so quiet. Well, I came home for lunch just in time to see her head for the switch bush so I managed to slip them each a dime and suggested that a few hours at the movie might give Mama time to simmer down!

You never could tell though what might strike Ellen's funny bone. One night Billy and Bill cut a section of inner tube and took turns looking at the big dipper through their homemade telescope. After a little while they got bored and decided to go wake the little girls and when the two of them innocently followed the boys out to see the stars, Bill held the inner tube while Billy poured a bucket of water from the fish pool into the funnel it made ... My, I never heard such squeals and screams. I thought Ellen might really tan their hides good and proper but, but just as I got primed to intervene, she busted out laughing and took off upstairs with the two little drowned rats, to put on dry nightgowns and sooth their hurt feelings with a sugar biscuit and chocolate milk and those rascal boys got off scott-free!

A big treat for those city kids was to be allowed to walk to town, all by themselves. They'd come by the store for peanuts and for the quarter I'd give them to spend at the five and ten cent store on their way to the picture show. In those depression days, the theatre owner would let any child without a dime get in for an egg, and I remember on one occasion Billy and Bill sneaked out of the house, each hiding an egg in his pocket so they could squander the money Ellen had given them on jawbreakers and bubble gum and still get in to see the cowboy picture.

And there was the time the little girls persuaded the boys to take them along without their Mama's permission. Ellen and Ann were straight out of the orchard where they loved to climb up and eat the ripe cherries by dipping them in salt. Ellen was grimy dirty, with her hair hanging in her face and her pinafore ripped and Ann, as usual, looked like she'd just stepped out of the tub.

After going about three blocks, stopping every few feet to yell at the girls to keep up and finally realizing that their short legs and bare feet were just not getting the job done, Billy told them they'd have to go on back home. Now, my Ellen was playing bridge down the street at Alma's and when she looked out the window and saw those two little girls, crossing Main Street all by themselves and looking like white trash to boot, she had a kernipshion fit! I was never sure whether it was the fear that they might get run over or her embarrassment over their appearance that got her so worked up but in any case there were no sugar biscuits that night!

Kate's Ellen did love to climb trees. Her favorite was the big maple outside the living room window that had limbs just like a step ladder and every time we couldn't find her, we'd go out and look up and there she'd be, sitting on the third or fourth limb up, with her pencil and tablet, either writing in her diary or making up a poem. I swear I hated to cut down that tree for that very reason, but when we decided to remodel the house, it just had to go.

Berto had hired a bunch of carpenters and tradesmen and had been busy around town building houses and a few business establishments and even a skating rink, so he had lots of ideas about how to go about this project. He even figured out a way we could all stay right on the property and not have to move while the **de**struction and **con**struction were under way.

In spite of having to use the privy out by the henhouse, Ellen and I were very comfortable in the room we fixed up over the smokehouse and even managed to stay good and warm from the fires built down below to smoke the hams. But Berto, Bess, and Ann had a little rougher go of it. We had torn off the back porch and moved it into the side yard to serve as a makeshift bungalow for them and even though it was boarded up and caulked pretty good, the wind still whistled through the cracks and, I do believe, that winter went down in the books as the coldest one ever in these parts. I can still remember hearing Cotton, Berto's white setter, coming up from his morning swim in the river, with the icicles that were hanging down under his belly clinking together!

But come summer, the worst was over and when the children came from Nashville, it was sorta like one long picnic. Ellen thought it was quite a lark, sleeping on two chairs pulled together with an ottoman in between, and the boys had cots set up with us up over the smokehouse. We ate many a watermelon in the side yard that summer and roasted a lot of wieners and marshmallows over the fire we built in a circle of rocks. The boys had plenty of scrap lumber to drive nails in and the girls found numerous nooks and crannies to use as houses for their dolls.

The day finally came when they delivered the four big reeded columns and as they raised them up there in front of our wonderful new home on the hill, I got kinda emotional, remembering where I'd come from to get to this place in my life and all I'd encountered along the way. We Badgers have been blessed, all right, and I remember hoping that those three children standing there, watching as this final touch was put on my particular dream, would someday share my gratitude to God for all He has made possible for this family.

No, you're not interrupting anything, Jacob. I was just sitting here, reading my Bible and thinking back ...

Nineteen

I guess by now you've caught on to the fact that my church and my Bible have always played a big part in my life. But I sure don't want you to get the idea that I carry the same love and respect for all the many preachers I've seen come and go over the years. In the Presbyterian scheme of things our McMinnville church was a way station ... we caught the preachers on the way up or on the way down ... and, you know, I believe I'll take my chances with those on the way down anyday! At least with them you have a chance to find out a little about what's coming your way.

I don't remember names as well as I used to, but a few of the men who filled our pulpit do stick in my mind. There was the one who not only refused to pay for the coal I delivered to the manse but flat out lied and told my grandaughter he'd already paid when, the next week, I sent her to the door to collect. And there was one young whippersnapper who believed in the laying on of hands ... especially when the one in need of prayerful intervention was a pretty young girl! I do remember one name ... Shadrach Summers. He was the fella who turned down our request to join the volunteer fire department and it was his garage that caught fire because he stored his gasoline cans where he shouldn't. Boy, did he whine when it took the boys fifteen minutes to arrive cause they'd had trouble starting up the fire truck. You'd have thought that particular "fiery furnace" had been visited on him by God instead of his own carelessness.

But we fell heir to some dandies, too. Like the preacher who once purposely mixed up the Biblical references he used in his sermon and then waited at the front door to see who'd correct him. And there was Brother Pardue (or was it Parsons?), a widower who made the best chicken soup in town, and when he'd arrive to console a grieving family or visit the sick and dying, he'd bring along this healing potion to add substance to his comforting words.

But my favorite of all the pastors who came our way was the one by the name of Samuel Whittemore. He was about sixty-two when he was called to our church and his days of flaming oratory were over and his evangelical skills were declining rapidly but he came to occupy a special place in our hearts nevertheless.

The havoc that the Depression wrought on this country was barely felt in Warren County. We didn't have folks jumping out of buildings ... I guess because the tallest building in town was just two and a half stories! ... and though our county poor house was full up we didn't have too many beggars on the street. A big portion of the thanks for this goes to Sam Whittemore.

You see, McMinnville's economy was not too broad based, being heavy into lumber and wood products. Our local companies, like McMinnville Manufacturing and the Rocky River Lumber Company, kept their doors open even while their wooden handles and hames piled up in the side lots, but that shoe company that had come down here from New York closed up shop at the first sign of trouble and high-tailed it back up north. That wouldn't have been so bad 'cept that in the beginning they had painted such a rosy picture of the company's future that a lot of folks in town sunk their savings into the stock that was selling so cheap. When they discovered the stock to be worth next to nothing it was too late to bail out . Those that could afford it just "took their lumps" and looked on it as a valuable lesson, but unfortunately a goodly number of those that found themselves looking at the worthless paper had been workers at the plant who were planning to retire on what supposedly was a sound investment, and in one fell swoop they found themselves without job or security.

One day when Brother Whittemore saw a little girl, shivering in the icy winds blowing down High Street, he put his own coat around her shoulders and walked with her to the place she called home. After talking to her parents and other victims of the plant closing who now found themselves destitute, he invited this family into his own home and with the pitifully small salary our church could afford to pay him, he bought food for others who were hungry and he got us to open the basement of the church to those who needed a place to get warm. You know the story in Matthew about the loaves and fishes? Well, before long half the folks in town were dropping by the church with a frying chicken, or a mess of greens, or a pair of outgrown shoes and a sweater, and Mr. Bass had found a way to hire a couple more men in his lumber yard and Jim Smoot had decided he really could use an extra hand to bring in the hay, and though we ate not quite as "high on the hog" as we'd been used to, we all managed to survive the depression in pretty good shape.

So you see, I might not recall the names of our finest pulpit orators, but I'll always remember Samuel Whittemore ... now there was a man of God.

Well, well, Jacob. Who's that you have with you? I think I would have known him on the street ... he's your spittin' image. Ellen always said of ours, "they're worth a million dollars and you couldn't get a nickel for either of them!" But seriously, you'll find that they are not only the source of life's greatest joys but occasionally, of its greatest heartaches.

Twenty

I never thought I'd rue the day I got the volunteer fire department started in McMinnville. Oh, I'm sure it has prevented the loss of property and, in some cases lives, but it sure had a dire consequence for our family.

It happened like this. One summer evening we were sitting in front of the radio, listening to Mr. Kaltenborn give the news, with Berto and me arguing about whether Roosevelt was a saint or sinner ... Berto maintaining that he was going to be the ruination of the country, and me contending he had shown what he was made of when he appointed Mr. Hull to the cabinet ... and the fire bell commenced to sound off. Ann jumped up and ran to the telephone to ask "Central" where the fire was while Berto went to get his hip boots and fireman's hat. You see, Berto had joined up with the group and could always be counted on to be among the first to arrive at the trouble spot.

This night the fire had started in the basement of the dry goods store on the square and had plenty of fodder to feed the flames and when we arrived ... (oh, yes ... we all went to watch ... don't know that it was morbid curiosity ... just a community happening that we didn't want to miss.) anyway, when we got there the smoke was pouring out the roof and it was obvious that the water had to be gotten up to the top floor to do any good. Berto volunteered to climb the ladder with an ax to break out one of the plate glass windows and to guide the fire hose into the building. The plan was OK but just as he had the ax raised, the window exploded outwards and a huge jagged piece of glass sliced across his hat and down the front of his face.

I'll never know how he was able to climb down the ladder with all that blood pouring from the open wound, but he did and only fainted when he saw the horrified looks on the faces of the bystanders. I almost passed out myself. But Bess was a "brick." She hollered for someone to get Dr. Smith and called for others to help get Berto over to the clinic, which fortunately was just down the street next to the Presbyterian Church. Dr. Smith got there straightaway and got all scrubbed up but when he looked at Berto he realized he couldn't use an ether mask because of the area that had to be stitched. We knew he was real allergic to all the pain killers like codeine and morphine so the operation had to be carried out with no anesthetic whatsoever.

How that boy stood it is a mystery cause they told me later that Dr. Smith took over a hundred stitches. For that matter I don't see how Bess stood it, either. Ellen had taken Ann on home and Bess and I sat in that little waiting room for what seemed like an eternity, listening to her husband and my son scream bloody murder, and when the doctor came out he was wringing wet. He admitted that he'd never in his career gone through anything that affected him like that but said he'd given Berto a tetanus shot and he seemed to be doing all right.

My legs were so watery that Bess had to drive me home but after picking up a few things she went right back to sit with Berto. It's good she did cause in the middle of the night he began yelling like a Banshee and grabbing at the bandages which were wrapped all around his head. Bess immediately figured out what was happening and called for the nurse and together they were able to quickly unwind all the dressings. We should have guessed that with all his other allergies he'd not be able to tolerate the tetanus serum and sure enough his head had swollen up to almost twice its regular size and the pressure of the bindings was causing excruciating pain.

Well, fortunately no infection set in and in time his face healed but he was left with terrible scars which drew his lip and indeed changed his entire expression. But trust Berto to make a joke of even that. When they removed the last of the bandages and Ellen saw him, she sorta teared up and Berto said, "Just look at it this way, Mama ... All these years I've been trying to whistle like Elmo Tanner ... now he's gonna wish he could whistle like me!"

Twenty-One

What? Do I remember Pearl Harbor? Like it was yesterday. I may forget where I put my glasses or my next-door neighbor's name but I'll never forget that Sunday. Kate, Will and the children had come up for the day and Will insisted on taking us all down to the Sedberry Hotel for dinner. It didn't suit Ellen too well but she agreed to the plan as long as we promised we'd come back home for dessert ... she'd just taken an apple cobbler out of the oven ... one made from those good Cardwell Mountain apples ... and no one put up much of a fight about that plan!

We walked in the house about one o'clock, full as ticks after stuffing ourselves with the Sedberry's country ham and squash casserole and I went over to turn on the radio. It was about time for the Sammy Kaye Serenade program (one of my favorites) but instead of the familiar music, we heard news-casters talking about bombs and sinking ships and our sailors being killed over in Hawaii. What a shock! Everyone had expected more trouble in Europe and those "in the know" predicted we'd have to jump in there sooner or later, but for little old Japan to up and kick our fannies was unthinkable.

Will shifted that big cigar he was always chewing on around in his mouth and said they'd best be getting on home. It was the general feeling that this was just the beginning of worse things to come ... as indeed it was ... and in times of trouble, folks just seem to head for their own front door like cows will head for the barn when they sense a storm is on the way.

For the next few years the whole country seemed to be turned inside out ... Changing from peacetime to preparing for war was unsettling, to say the least. All metals and leather and rubber and half the stuff we ate was needed for the armed forces and while some people whined and complained, most of us were glad to make do with shortages and rationing. I learned to drink my iced tea with saccharin ... though I kept knocking out the bottom of my glass trying to dissolve those durn little tablets! ... and Ellen began cooking with honey instead of sugar. And, you know, our bees seemed to sense their importance, cause, during those years, when I'd rob the hives, I could swear there was twice as much honey as before!

Our ration stamps pretty well covered our needs as we had two families' allotments to count on, and we raised a lot of our own food. Helping out neighbors who were less well provisioned kept me busy delivering Ellen's baskets ... that is, as long as the old black chevy held up. We did have access to more gasoline than most folks. Because of my farms I had a "C" sticker ... what was that? Oh, the sticker you were given, whether "A," "B," or "C," determined how much gas you were allowed, and doctors and farmers and such as used their cars and tractors in ways to benefit the community were given the most.

Getting new tires was out of the question, so when one got thin or blew out you got a retread. I could name you a fella in this town today that has a fine house and fancy ways who made a small fortune dealing in shoddy retreads and black market gas. (I never did hold with taking advantage of other's misfortunes, and the first time this man's application for a loan came up before the bank board, I personally convinced my fellow directors to turn it down. The bank lost a customer but I don't believe a one of us was ever sorry.)

I watched many a Warren County youngster go off to fight in that war ... some to Europe and some to the Pacific ... and we considered ourselves mighty lucky when the war ended before Berto (Oh, did I say "Berto"? I meant "Billy".) before he had to go overseas with his Naval aviation unit. Now that young fella that later married my grandaughter over in Nashville, (that's right. His name is Tom) well, he spent right smart time in the Pacific, and Johnny, the one that married Berto's girl, he was in the Navy, too, but the war was over before he had to leave the country.

But the picture that comes most readily to my mind when you speak of that war is that of our front yard, all the way from where the driveway splits at the top of the hill, clear down to the highway, cram full of soldiers from Camp Forrest over in Tullahoma, with their trucks, and tents, and big guns. You see, I'd given my permission for them to camp there during their summer maneuvers .... I felt that was the least I could do. Ellen was sharing the vegetables from her garden and the eggs from her hens with the neighbors, Bess was rolling bandages down at the church, and Ann was dancing with the officers on Saturday nights at the Sedberry, and I remember thinking, "all that is well and good but here's my chance to really make a contribution."

Most of the soldiers were real nice and polite ... their captain even came up and apologized when they set the grass on fire and burned up Ellen's lilac bushes ... and when the trucks mired up in the bottom after one really hard rain, they smoothed it all over so that the ruts wouldn't upset the hay rake. But that one Sunday when Ellen and I drove down the hill on our way to church and I looked over and saw a bunch of them drinking whiskey and playing cards ... right there in plain view ... and on the Sabbath ... I've got to say that for an instant I regretted my patriotic gesture. Now, wouldn't you think those boys' mamas would have taught them better? Fortunately it wasn't too long after that that they finished building their pontoon bridge across the river and broke camp and moved on up into the mountains. Can't say I was too sorry to see the last of them, but when they were packing up and I saw two baby-faced young privates come running up to bring Ellen a scrawny little lilac bush, I must admit to feeling a bit choked up. Then the next day when I saw the newly dug hole in Mrs.Henry's yard down the street,I had to laugh ... and I remember thinking, "with that kind of ingenuity, our boys are gonna come out OK in this conflict!"

No. I was just sitting here going through some picture albums. Come on in and I'll ask Ellen to get us some iced tea.

Twenty-Two

Just look here at this ... can you believe Kate talked me into getting all gussied up like this for Ellen's wedding? But then, just look at my Ellen ... pretty as a picture sure nuff! But I can't for the life of me figure out why they have to make such a to-do out of getting married over there in Nashville though. Now my grandaughter, Ann, was a lot more sensible. When she and Johnny married they planned the whole shebang right here at home. Ann came down the stairway, looking like a princess and the two of them stood right there in front of the mantle and tied the knot.

But nothing would do Kate but to go the whole nine yards ... announcement in the papers, fancy invitations, big church with flowers all over everywhere, and a party at their house after the ceremony with folks streaming through I'd never seen before and didn't much care if I never saw again! I remember it was hot as blue blazes and that starched collar 'bout cut my neck in two.

Once during the evening I escaped to a back room to sit in front of a fan and ran into Pete Hudson who had the same idea ... he's the father of the young man that was marrying Ellen ... and we had a good time talking about Sparta and White County. Would you believe it was in his father's law office where I met Mr.Hull those many years ago, and Pete says some of his folks are buried over at the Mt.Pisgah churchyard and he's seen the Badger name on some of the gravestones there. He says most of the folks in the cemetery are descended from some man named Knowles.

Now wouldn't it be something if the bride and groom turned out to be some kind of kin?

Oh, it;s you, Jacob. Come in ... let me turn this television set off. They tell me I keep it turned up so loud it drives them all away ... not a bad idea sometimes!

Twenty-Three

What's this? Another baby? It appears every time I turn around someone's putting a baby up in my lap to take a picture. How many's this now? My, each one seems to get handsomer than the last. No wonder they call them "great" and "grand"!

But you know, I can't help but think of what Ellen's grandpa said one time. All the children and their children had descended on them for some occasion or the other (and in Ellen's family that added up to a passel of folks!) and after a long day of eating, talking, romping, and wading in the creek, and as the last wagon rolled down the drive, Mammy said, "Ain't it gonna be lonesome without the chillun around?" and Pappy thought a minute and said, "Yeh, but it sho will be a happy lonesome.!"

Hello there, Jacob. Come in here and tell me about this Mississippi gal I hear Billy's gonna marry. Every Mississippi miss I've ever known was a sure 'nuff beauty. What! You don't know Billy?

You'll have to excuse this old man, Jacob. After all these years I guess I've got to thinking of you as one of "us!"

Twenty-Four

They've started hounding me about selling my car. Pshaw! They don't fool me. They think I'm getting too old to drive. I can still drive better than all those young fools that dart in and out and around me when I'm driving down Main Street on my way to town, minding my own business. Why those hoodlums probably don't even know where they're going and won't know a soul when they get there!

But, between you and me, I did run up on the curb and ruin a tire the other day when I was turning into Smithville Street on my way to the Fair Board meeting. Bob Wilson was at the meeting ... the one that runs the filling station down there on the corner ... and he got it fixed for me so's I could drive it home that night. And once last month I found myself out on the Viola Road and couldn't for the life of me remember how I'd gotten there.

Maybe it is time to give up my car ... it's just that I want to be the one to make that decision.

Twenty-Five

Ellen died last night ... When I woke up this morning only her body was there ... She had gone. How can this be? Why, it goes against everything we'd talked about those nights after the dishes were done, when we'd sit on the front porch and rock and discuss how she'd manage after I'd gone ... I was supposed to go first ... And now she's left me ... We never planned how I'd manage without her ....

All right, Jacob. Come on in. But I really don't feel much like talking today.

Twenty-Six

You'll never know just what lonesome is till you bury your best friend and only love in the same grave. And, can you believe they buried Ellen to the left of the spot they saved for me there on the cemetery lot, when she'd been my right arm for sixty-seven years?

I still catch myself going to the kitchen to tell her something or looking up each time the back door slams. I expect to see her walking in, pushing her hair off her forehead, carrying a big bunch of sweet peas or a mess of turnip greens, and laughing about the latest mischief the little boys next door have gotten into. But there's weeds in the garden and the hens have about stopped laying and its all I can do to make myself get up in the morning.

I know they say the Lord never places burdens on a person's back lest he can carry the load, but just last night they came in to tell me that Berto had to go in the hospital over in Nashville for some tests ... first I'd known he was having problems. At this point I'm awfully afraid neither my back nor my spirit is up to carrying the load.

Twenty-Seven

Ellen, Ellen ... Come in here.

You're not Ellen.

Bess? Bess, who?

Well, who's that hollering?

Berto? No that's not a child's cry. That's someone really hurting.

Bone cancer? How'd he get that?

Well, can't Dr.Mulligan do something?

Dr. who?

Never heard of him.

Well, call Kate if you can't find Ellen.

In Nashville? What's she doing over there?

OK, then. Bring me some of that peppermint candy and my Bible and tell that man to hush up and go on home ... I want to take a nap....

Twenty-Eight

Who are all these people milling around in here? and who is this black haired girl who keeps bringing me food I don't want? I want some of Ellen's cornbread and buttermilk.

Where is Ellen anyway?

Maybe we'd better call the sheriff ... there are a lot of tough looking men down there on the road and some of them are carrying guns.

I don't like this place.

I want to go home.

I'm so tired ....

Epilogue

Four years after Felix died NASA sent a man to the moon … and when he got there, he didn't know a soul!